BOOK TWO
BASED ON THE HIT TV SHOW 'THE AVENGERS'

STEED and Mrs PEEL

ILLUSTRATED BY
Ian GIBSON
WRITTEN BY
GRANT MORRISON · THE GOLDEN GAME
ANNE CAULFIELD · DEADLY RAINBOW

ECLIPSE BOOKS · ACME PRESS

STEED and Mrs PEEL Book Two

Published by
Eclipse Comics,
P.O. Box 1099, Forestville, California 95436 USA
and
Acme Press, 391 Coldharbour Lane, London SW9 8LQ UK.

Writers:
Grant Morrison
Anne Caulfield
Artist:
Ian Gibson
Letterer:
Ellie de Ville
Designer:
Rian Hughes
Editor:
Dick Hansom
Back Cover Photographer:
John R Ward
Consulting Editors:
Dave Rogers
Catherine Yronwode
Michael Bennent

"An Elephant Never Forgets"
Titheradge/Schumann/Griffiths/Erkin
© Ascherberg, Hopwood and Crew
Reproduced by Warner Chappell Music Ltd.

ISBN 1-870084-81-0

Printed in the USA.

part three:

FOX & GEESE

FOX & GEESE

part three:

I'M GLAD YOU COULD MAKE IT, MR STEED.

THE PALAMEDES CLUB

MR BIRD SPOKE **VERY** HIGHLY OF YOU BEFORE HE ... AH ... **PASSED AWAY.**

IT'S ON **HIS** RECOMMENDATION THAT WE'VE INVITED YOU HERE FOR THIS PRELIMINARY **INTERVIEW.**

AND YOU ARE?

CALL ME **CHANCE**, MR STEED.

MR CHANCE? HOW **APPROPRIATE.**

NOT REALLY. ALL THE PALAMEDES CLUB SECRETARIES HAVE BEEN KNOWN AS CHANCE.

IT'S SOMETHING OF A TRADITION.

REALLY?

I HADN'T REALISED THE CLUB WAS OLD ENOUGH FOR TRADITION.

OH YES. IT WAS ORIGINALLY FOUNDED IN 1878.

I AM RIGHT, AREN'T I, MR WOLLOW?

OH YES. 1878.

WE GO BACK A VERY LONG WAY AND SOME OF OUR MEMBERS HAVE BEEN VERY DISTINGUISHED IN- DEED. YES.

THE CLUB WAS DIS- BANDED DURING THE SECOND WORLD WAR AND WAS ONLY RE- VIVED RECENTLY BY ADMIRAL FANSHAWE AND THE ...UM... OTHERS. GOD REST THEIR SOULS.

BEFORE WE PROCEED TO THE PAPER- WORK, I HOPE YOU WON'T MIND SUBMITTING TO A SMALL TEST, MR STEED.

A TEST?

I'M GAME.

SPLENDID! IT'S JUST A FORMALITY REALLY.

TRADITION?

THAT'S IT. TRADITION.

THERE ARE CERTAIN ATTRIBUTES WHICH CANNOT BE TAUGHT. CERTAIN QUALITIES WHICH ARE, SHALL WE SAY, THE PRIVILEGE OF THE FEW.

WELL THEN, WHAT MORE CAN I **SAY**, MR STEED? YOU'VE **PASSED** THE FIRST TEST WITH FLYING COLOURS.

CONGRATULATIONS.

THE NEXT MOVE IS FOR US TO INVITE YOU DOWN TO OUR **HOUSE** IN THE COUNTRY, WHERE WE HOLD THE FULL **INAUGURATION** CEREMONY.

BEFORE YOU LEAVE, IT'S OUR CUSTOM TO PRESENT EVERYONE WHO MAKES IT THIS FAR WITH A SMALL **TOKEN**.

WOULD YOU BE KIND ENOUGH TO PRESENT MR STEED WITH HIS COMMEMORATIVE **DARTBOARD**, MR WOLLOW?

NOW, BEFORE I **FORGET**: WHAT WAS THE NAME OF THIS **GAME** YOU'VE DEVISED, MR STEED?

I'M SORRY, DIDN'T I **TELL** YOU?

IT'S **ROOKS AND RAVENS**.

STILL INTERESTED?

THEY SEEMED VERY **DISCONCERTED** WHEN I MENTIONED ROOKS AND RAVENS.

'YOU'RE GOING TO DIE! YOU'RE GOING TO DIE! UNLESS YOU PLAY THE GAME. YOU HEARD THE ROOKS AND RAVENS CRY, SO YOU'VE ONLY YOURSELVES TO BLAME.'

THE GOLDEN GAME

Reynard's Rid—

I CHECKED AT THE LIBRARY: THIS BOOK WAS NEVER **PUB-LISHED.**

THIS SEEMS TO BE THE **ONLY** COPY.

WHY WOULD SOMEONE GO TO THE TROUBLE OF PRINTING UP A BOOK JUST TO SEND IT TO **ME?** AND WHAT DOES ALL THIS HAVE TO DO WITH THE **HANGMAN** NUCLEAR DEFENSE PRO-GRAMME?

IT ALL SEEMS LIKE SOME HUGE...

GAME, STEED?

EXACTLY. I'VE TO VISIT THEM TOMORROW AT SOME PLACE CALLED **WADDING-TON HALL.** MY 'INAUGURATION CEREMONY'.

I HOPE YOU'VE PREPARED A **SPEECH.**

WELCOME TO WADDINGTON HALL.

MR CHANCE! I HOPE I'M NOT LATE!

NOT YET.

DON'T THINK WE HAVEN'T SEEN THROUGH YOUR LITTLE DECEPTION, MR STEED.

SEVERAL YEARS AGO, YOU SEE, WE HAD SOMEONE ELSE APPLY FOR MEMBERSHIP WITH A GAME CALLED ROOKS AND RAVENS.

THIS GAME, IN AN ATTEMPT TO ELIMINATE THE ELEMENT OF COMPETITION, WAS BASED AROUND PRINCIPLES OF COOPERATION.

WHAT AN EXTRAORDINARY COINCIDENCE.

YES. THE GAME'S INVENTOR APPLIED TO THE PALAMEDES CLUB AND WAS REJECTED.

APPARENTLY, THE GAME WAS VIRTUALLY UNPLAYABLE.

YOU MAY, HOWEVER, BE FAMILIAR WITH THE NAME OF THE INVENTOR.

HILARY FOX.

GOOD HEAVENS! NOT OLD 'FOUR-EYES' FOX?

'FOUR-EYES' FOX FROM ETON?

EENI, MEENI, MACKER, ACKER AIR, I, DONNAL MACKER CHICA, PICA, WOLLA, WOLLA

EXACTLY.

REYNARD THE FOX.

OM, POM PUSH!

OH, BAD SHOW. IT SEEMS YOU'RE IT, MR STEED.

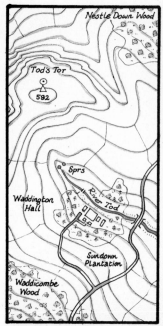

'THE BIRDS CAME HOME TO ROOST TODAY
OUR GAME IS ALL BUT DONE.
WHERE'S REYNARD FOUND?
HE'S GONE TO GROUND,
BENEATH THE SETTING SUN.'

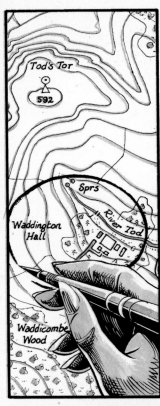

WADDINGTON HALL.

STEED!

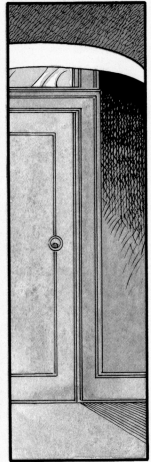

ALL THE WORLD'S A BOARD MY DEAR. IT'S ALWAY'S BEEN THE SAME. NOW'S YOUR TURN TO START TO LEARN TO PLAY THE GOLDEN GAME.

ALL I CAN TELL YOU IS THAT YOU AND I ARE GOING **UP** IN THE WORLD.

FOLLOW ME, MR STEED.

SO, HILARY FOX WAS REJECTED FROM THE CLUB AND HE DECIDED TO **KILL** THE FOUR CHARTER MEMBERS FOR RE-VENGE?

SOUNDS LIKE A VERY POOR **LOSER**.

AND NOW HE'S GOT **YOU** WORKING FOR HIM.

DOING **WHAT** EXACTLY?

YOU DON'T UNDER-STAND, MR STEED. HE'S PROVED TO US HOW EASILY AND HOW CLEVERLY HE CAN KILL US.

WE **HAD** TO DO WHAT HE WANTED: IMPERSONATING FANSHAWE TO KIDNAP MISS KING, PRINTING THE **BOOK**. WE **HAD** TO.

IF THEY'D ONLY LET HIM **IN**, NONE OF THIS WOULD HAVE HAPPENED.

I DON'T KNOW WHY THEY DIDN'T: HILARY FOX IS THE FINEST **GAMESMAN** I'VE EVER ENCOUNTERED.

HE'S ALSO FAIRLY **UNSUFFERABLE**, FROM WHAT I REMEMBER.

WHERE DOES THE **HANGMAN** DEFENSE PROGRAMME FIT INTO THIS GRAND SCHEME?

THAT'S **ENOUGH**.

I'M AFRAID THE FAMILY LUCK'S RUN OUT.

I'M SORRY, MR STEED.

WE HAVE NO **CHOICE**.

YOU'VE HAD A GOOD RUN OF IT BUT LIFE IS NEVER DEPENDABLE. ONE MINUTE WE'RE CLIMBING THE **LADDER** WITHOUT A CARE IN THE WORLD...

AND THE NEXT WE'RE SLIDING DOWN THE **SNAKE** !

WELL, IF IT ISN'T OLD **STEED**. STEED THE **CHEAT**.

WELCOME TO MY **PARLOUR**, STEED. I'VE WAITED RATHER A LONG TIME FOR THIS.

HILARY ? 'FOUR-EYES', IS THAT **YOU** ?

DON'T YOU **DARE** CALL ME 'FOUR-EYES' EVER AGAIN ! IT'S **MISTER** FOX TO YOU !

64

WADDINGTON HALL, YOU SAY?

YES, THAT'S RIGHT. WADDINGTON HALL.

YOU DO KNOW IT?

COURSE I DO! THAT'S WHERE ALL THEM QUEER TYPES GO WITH THEIR GAMES.

GET SOME OF THEM IN HERE SOMETIMES, ASKING FOR A GO ON THE SHOVE HA'PENNY TABLE...

ALL I REALLY WANT TO KNOW IS THE BEST WAY TO GET THERE FROM HERE.

THERE'S A SIDE ROAD ABOUT HALF A MILE FROM HERE ON YOUR LEFT. GO TWO MILE UP THAT ROAD AND YOU CAN'T MISS IT.

REPORTER, ARE YOU? I BET YOU'RE FROM ONE OF THOSE SUNDAY NEWSPAPERS. I COULD TELL YOU A FEW STORIES, IF YOU MAKE IT WORTH MY WHILE.

GIVE ME AN HOUR AND I'LL HAVE SOME STORIES FOR YOU.

WELL DONE, STEED. STILL AS SMUG AND COCKSURE AS EVER.

PERHAPS YOU MIGHT JUST SURVIVE LONG ENOUGH TO TAKE PART IN THE **GOLDEN GAME**, AFTER ALL.

WHAT EXACTLY **IS** THE GOLDEN GAME?

THEY WOULDN'T LET ME JOIN THEIR STUPID **CLUB**. THEY SAID **ROOKS** AND **RAVENS** WOULDN'T WORK. STORY OF MY **LIFE**.

SO I'VE DEVISED THE GAME TO END ALL GAMES.

DOES THIS HAVE ANYTHING TO DO WITH THE **HANGMAN** PROGRAMME?

OH, GO TO THE TOP OF THE CLASS STEED! THAT'S WHERE YOU AL-WAYS **WERE**, WASN'T IT?

THE GAME BEGINS WITH A ROLL OF THE THERMONUCLEAR **DICE**. THINK ABOUT **THAT** WHILE YOU PLAY THE **NEXT** GAME.

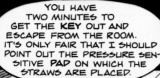

JACKSTRAWS.

YOU HAVE TWO MINUTES TO GET THE **KEY** OUT AND ESCAPE FROM THE ROOM. IT'S ONLY FAIR THAT I SHOULD POINT OUT THE PRESSURE SEN-SITIVE **PAD** ON WHICH THE STRAWS ARE PLACED.

ONE FALSE MOVE, ONE MISPLACED STRAW AND THERE'LL BE A NEW STAR IN HEAVEN TONIGHT.

CAREFUL, STEED.

THAT'S IT.

NEXT ISSUE – PART 4: HANGMAN

1

3

5

6

DEADLY RAINBOW

9

GOODBYE FOREVER THEN, MRS PEEL.

WHY DO I FEEL RATHER PLEASED THAT EMMA PEEL MARRIED SOMEONE EXACTLY LIKE ME?

WE SHOULDN'T HAVE DONE IT. POOR OLD STEED'S GOING TO WONDER ABOUT THAT ONE FOR A LONG TIME.

GOODBYES ARE ALWAYS DREADFUL—I THINK IT HELPS TO ADD A LITTLE TWIST OF SURPRISE.

LIKE SAYING 'GOODBYE, I'LL BE FLYING FOR THREE DAYS'... AND TAKING THREE YEARS?

I PROMISE I'D HAVE SENT YOU A POSTCARD... IF I'D KNOWN WHAT NAME TO SIGN.

NEVER MIND. I KEPT MYSELF BUSY... COOKING, SEWING...

...FIGHTING INTERNATIONAL VILLAINS.

WHERE ARE YOU TAKING ME, NOW I'VE ESCAPED FROM A LIFE OF ADVENTURE?

REMEMBER PRINGLE ON SEA?

CALL ME ROMANTIC IF YOU LIKE ...

WE SPENT THE FIRST NIGHT OF OUR HONEYMOON THERE, BEFORE THE ROUND THE WORLD HELICOPTER RACE.

I THINK I'D RATHER JUST CALL YOU PEEL ... IN CASE YOU FORGET WHO YOU ARE AGAIN.

BY THE WAY, DON'T BE TOO SURE YOU'VE ESCAPED A LIFE OF ADVENTURE, MRS PEEL ...

IN PRINGLE ON SEA?

BUT NOTHING HAS HAPPENED HERE SINCE THERE WAS A TOTAL ECLIPSE OF THE SUN A HUNDRED YEARS AGO ...

PRINGLE ON SEA

... AND I THINK THEY MADE THAT UP, IN A DESPERATE BID TO SEEM EXCITING.

THAT'S WHY WE'RE ONLY STAYING HERE OVER-NIGHT.

THE LEOPARD PEOPLE ARE THE ONES WHO NEED ALL THE HELP THEY CAN GET.

WE'RE GOING TO SPEND OUR SECOND HONEYMOON IN THE AMAZON JUNGLE?

DON'T YOU WANT TO GO?

TRY AND STOP ME, PEEL!

BESIDES, I THINK THE JUNGLE WILL BE VERY GOOD FOR ME — IT'LL KEEP ME AWAY FROM DIABOLICAL MASTERMINDS...

.... I COULD BECOME A COMPLETELY REFORMED CHARACTER.

I DOUBT IT.

OH REALLY? I WAS SO HOPING TO LIVE HAPPILY EVER AFTER AS THE DEMURE WIFE OF AN AIR ACE HERO.

WAVING A TEAR-STAINED HANKY AS YOU DASH OFF TO BE BIG AND BRAVE WHILE I STAY AT HOME AND...

...EMBROIDER MORE HANKIES WHAT BLISS! WHAT AN INTERESTING LIFE!

WHAT A SHAME YOU'D BE HOPELESS AT IT.

MR AND MRS PEEL! HOW WONDERFUL TO SEE YOU AGAIN. WHAT'LL IT BE?

JUST A ROOM FOR NOW. OUR OLD ONE, IF POSSIBLE.

OF COURSE, YOUR ROOM'S FREE.

BIT OF TROUBLE WITH THE OLD BACK, SO 'FRAID I CAN'T HELP WITH THE CASES.

NOT TO WORRY, MY HUSBAND CAN MANAGE.

WE'VE GOT VISITORS...

14

GLAD YOU COULD MAKE IT, STEED. BIT OF AN *OCCURENCE*, OLD CHAP...

...IN DINGLE... NO-*PRINGLE* ON SEA! APPEARS A TEAM OF SURVEYORS FOR A NEW MOTORWAY WERE SENT DOWN TO MEASURE THE LIE OF THE LAND THERE AND...UM... DISAPPEARED OFF THE FACE OF THE EARTH.

CHAPS SENT TO LOOK FOR *THEM*, ALSO... DISAPPEARED. FOUL PLAY SUSPECTED.

SEEMS RATHER AN *EXTREME* METHOD OF CONSERVING THE COUNTRYSIDE.

I SENT DOWN A COUPLE OF OUR CHAPS, JONES AND CASEY, UNDERCOVER AS MEMBERS OF A VINTAGE STEAM ENGINE RALLY THAT VISITS PRINGLE EVERY SUMMER AND...

THEY'VE DISAPPEARED?

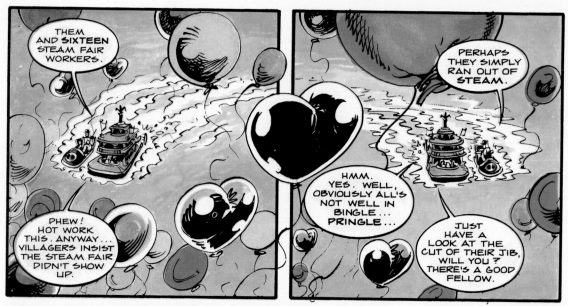

MORE RAINBOWS? WHERE'S THE . . .

IT'S A STRANGE THING FOR PRINGLE TO TAKE UP WITH.

THE ONLY PEOPLE KNOWN TO WORSHIP THE RAINBOW ARE . . .

THE INCAS!

WHAT THE . . .?

EMMA!

PEEL!

WE DIDN'T COVER THIS IN FLYING SCHOOL. ANY POINTERS?

FIGHT DIRTY!

17

WHATEVER IT WAS, I'M NOT GOING TO LET IT PUT ME OFF A CREAM TEA ON THE VILLAGE GREEN.

YOUR LIP'S BLEEDING.

GOT A HANKY?

WITH EMBROIDERY OR WITHOUT?

OH!

WELL, THAT'S RATHER CLOTTED THE CREAM.

YES, I FIND IT'S MARVELLOUS EXERCISE FOR THE BICEPS... HOLD ON A MOMENT... ...THERE'S SOMETHING...

hello? hello?

YES? CAN I HELP YOU?

NOT LIS-PICCHU

DOESN'T MAKE A SCRAP OF SENSE TO ME, OLD CHAP. YOU MUST HAVE THE WRONG ADDRESS...

PERHAPS YOU WERE LOOKING FOR AN ARK?

21

TO BE CONTINUED